D1710382

AMERICAN CARS

THROUGH THE DECADES

American Cars of the 1970s

Craig Cheetham

GARETH STEVENS
GS
PUBLISHING
A Member of the WRC Media Family of Companies

Please visit our web site at: **www.garethstevens.com**
For a free color catalog describing Gareth Stevens Publishing's
list of high-quality books and multimedia programs,
call 1-800-542-2595 (USA) or 1-800-387-3178 (Canada).
Gareth Stevens Publishing's fax: (414) 332-3567.

Library of Congress Cataloging-in-Publication Data

Cheetham, Craig.
    American cars of the 1970s / Craig Cheetham.
      p. cm. — (American cars through the decades)
    Includes bibliographical references and index.
    ISBN-13: 978-0-8368-7726-7 (lib. bdg.)
    1. Automobiles—United States—History. I. Title.
  TL23.C442   2007
  629.2220973'09047—dc22   2006051060

This North American edition first published in 2007 by
Gareth Stevens Publishing
A Member of the WRC Media Family of Companies
330 West Olive Street, Suite 100
Milwaukee, WI 53212 USA

Copyright © 2007 Amber Books Ltd.

Produced by Amber Books Ltd., Bradley's Close,
74–77 White Lion Street, London N1 9PF, U.K.

Project Editor: Michael Spilling
Design: Joe Conneally

Gareth Stevens managing editor: Valerie J. Weber
Gareth Stevens editor: Alan Wachtel
Gareth Stevens art direction: Tammy West
Gareth Stevens cover design: Dave Kowalski
Gareth Stevens production: Jessica Yanke and Robert Kraus

Illustrations and photographs copyright International Masters
Publishers AB/Aerospace–Art-Tech

Printed in the United States of America

1 2 3 4 5 6 7 8 9 10 10 09 08 07 06

Table of Contents

AMC AMX

*The AMX was a **muscle car**, but it was unusual for American cars of its time because of its small size.*

The AMX had just two seats.

The sloping rear made the AMX look like a **hatchback**, but it was actually a two-door **coupe**.

One of the options on the AMX was the "performance hood." The hood had air scoops in it and a bulge in the middle.

The car's chrome sides had **vents** in them to allow air to pass through.

Only 14 feet (4.2 meters) long, the AMX was one of the smallest American cars on sale at the time.

It was smaller than most muscle cars, but the AMC AMX had a powerful engine, and it held the road well.

1968

AMC announces its AMX "compact muscle car," which goes on sale the following year.

1971

After slow sales, the company downgrades the AMX, making the interior **trim** more basic. The 1971 model (below) is sought after today for its sleek styling.

AMC (American Motors Corporation) designed the AMX — a two-seater high-performance car with a 390-cubic-inch (6,390-cc) **V-8** engine — to compete with the Chevrolet Corvette. The car first appeared in the late 1960s, and AMC believed that its small size would attract buyers. The engine was the most powerful made by AMC at the time. It gave out 315 **horsepower**, enabling it to match its rivals.

Limited Success

The AMX was fast and could grip difficult mountain roads well. The car was never a success, however. Good performance meant little because drivers preferred bigger cars. From 1968 to 1973, fewer than 20,000 AMXs were sold. Today, because it is rare, the AMX is sought after by **classic** car collectors.

UNDER THE SKIN

Power brakes and a strong **suspension** helped the AMX handle the huge power from its engine.

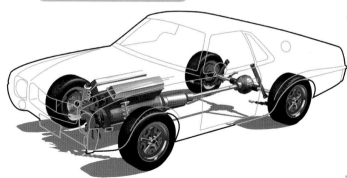

5

Bricklin SV-1

The Bricklin SV-1 was a sports car that also offered good safety features. This made it the first car of its kind.

The car's doors were hinged at the top. When opened, they looked like a bird's wings.

The whole front bumper of the Bricklin SV-1 was spring-loaded to absorb any crash damage at low speeds.

Like the Chevrolet Corvette, the SV-1 was made out of **fiberglass** to keep it from rusting.

Inside, all of the surfaces were padded and filled with foam to protect the passengers in a crash.

The SV-1's safety bumper stuck out from the car's front and gave it an awkward look.

1973
Businessman Malcolm Bricklin announces his new "Safety Vehicle" and says it will be a "big thing."

1975
After building fewer than 4,500 cars, Bricklin closes its factory.

The Bricklin SV-1 is one of the most interesting cars ever built. The SV part of the name stood for "safety vehicle." The car's makers wanted to see if drivers were interested in a sports car with a design that offered good safety features.

ideas, but the Bricklin was not well made. Because it broke down a lot, few people bought one. After two years of very slow sales, the company stopped making it.

Safety First
The design was clever. The SV-1 had doors that opened upward, a padded interior, and bumpers that pushed into the body in low-speed accidents to reduce the force of a crash. These were all good

UNDER THE SKIN

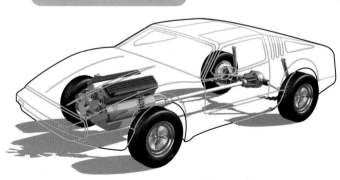

The fiberglass body covers a strong steel **chassis**, similar to that of a Chevrolet Corvette.

Chevrolet Camaro SS396

Chevrolet's new car for 1970 was the Camaro SS396. Its body was rounder and smoother than the original Camaro.

The SS396 had sports mirrors and a black radiator **grille**. It also had high-back bucket seats to keep the driver in place at high speeds.

For the first time, the Camaro has round taillights, like those on the Corvette.

The small back window looked cool, but it made it difficult for drivers to see properly when backing up.

Chevrolet planned to make a **convertible** Camaro, but it never appeared. All Camaros were hardtops.

Its softer, rounder nose made the Camaro more **aerodynamic**.

From the moment it appeared, the Camaro SS396 won praise for its styling.

MILESTONES

1970
Chevrolet unveils its new line of Camaro SS models, including the SS396.

1972
The company stops making the SS line.

Chevrolet launched its new Camaro in February 1970. Thanks to its rounded nose and wide rear wheel arches, it was an instant design classic. Its body looked so smooth that the company continued to make cars with the same shape well into the 1980s, with only minor changes.

Top Model

The SS396 model was second only to Chevrolet's trophy car, the Z28, which first appeared in 1971. The Z28 performed better on race circuits, but the SS396 was more powerful. With a large engine that was easy to tune for better performance, the SS396 could race the quarter mile in less than fourteen seconds. This made it popular with **drag racers**.

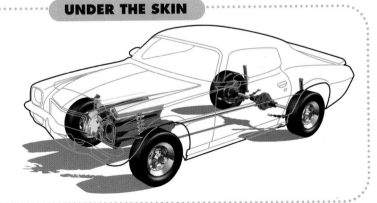

UNDER THE SKIN

All Camaros came with a strong suspension that included stiffened springs and shock absorbers.

9

Chevrolet Chevelle SS454

As the 1970s began, Chevrolet launched its most powerful sedan ever, the Chevelle SS.

The stripes on the car's hood and trunk were either black or white, depending on the main color of the car.

When the car was moving fast, a flap in the hood opened to suck extra air into the engine to cool it down.

Dual **exhaust pipes** came out below the rear fender.

All Chevelle SS models had steel wheels. They were black with polished chrome.

The Chevelle SS454 was as powerful as it looked. It could race quarter of a mile in 13.7 seconds.

1970

General Motors lifts its ban on big engines and produces its wildest muscle cars yet, including the Chevelle SS454. This included the rare and superpowerful LS-6 model (pictured below).

1973

The company launches a new, less powerful Chevelle.

In the mid-1960s, General Motors was cautious about building muscle cars, because muscle cars were fast and thought to be dangerous. However, by the end of the 1960s, General Motors had started building more muscle cars, because that was what buyers wanted.

Plain Powerhouse

In 1970, the company finally offered a car with a huge engine. The Chevelle SS had a 454-cubic-inches (7,440-cc) engine that put out 450 horsepower — even more power than muscle cars such as the Ford Mustang and Dodge Charger 500.

The engine was so heavy that it needed a suspension with very stiff front springs to carry the weight.

UNDER THE SKIN

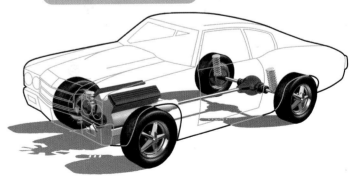

The Chevelle had a heavy-duty rear suspension to cope with the car's powerful engine.

11

Chevrolet Cosworth Vega

The Cosworth Vega was Chevrolet's answer to imported Japanese and European cars. But was it as good as they were?

Cosworth Vegas were made in small numbers and came only in black with gold trim.

The cabin was also black and gold. Each car had a plaque on the dash showing its serial number.

The Vega had marker lights at the front and rear to help other drivers see it on the road.

The Vega was based on the European Opel Manta, although much of its style came from the bigger Chevrolet Camaro.

So few Cosworth Vegas were built that they are highly valued by collectors today.

1971

Chevrolet introduces the Vega, but the car never really catches on.

1975

The company launches the Cosworth Vega model. It produces fewer than 5,000 of them because the car does not sell well.

In the mid 1970s, a fuel crisis made drivers think more about how much gas their cars used. As a result, big V-8 engines became less popular. To meet buyers' needs, car companies made cars that used less fuel.

122-cubic-inch (1,999-cc) engine that Cosworth used in Lotus **Formula One** cars. Electronic **fuel injection** made the Cosworth Vega one of the most advanced cars in the United States at the time.

Advanced Engine

For Chevrolet, the Vega was the solution, but people criticized its four-**cylinder** engine for being slow and noisy. To improve the Vega, Chevrolet asked for help from the British company Cosworth, which built racing-car engines. The result was the Cosworth Vega, which had the

UNDER THE SKIN

The Cosworth Vega's advanced wishbone front suspension was similar to the suspensions used in many European cars of the time.

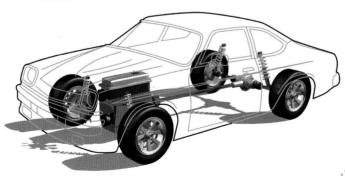

13

Dodge Coronet Super Bee

The Coronet was the last large muscle car built by Dodge.

The thick stripe on the rear of the car had the words "Super Bee" in the center.

The Coronet's front end had two separate grilles, one around each pair of headlights.

The Coronet's suspension was very simple, making it a difficult car to drive quickly around corners.

Drilled steel wheels with chrome on the rims came with the car.

The car's rear end looked like the back of the Dodge Charger, but the Coronet was much bigger.

Its powerful engine let the Super Bee race the quarter mile in under fourteen seconds.

1967

Dodge introduces the Coronet (pictured below).

1970

Dodge introduces the Coronet Super Bee, which features a redesigned grille and a four-light front end.

Dodge was known for its high-performance cars because the Dodge Charger had won many **NASCAR** races. The larger Coronet, on the other hand, was not meant for racing — but that did not stop Dodge from making it into a muscle car for the road.

coupe, sedan, and convertible models. No matter the model, its large hood and loud paint made the Super Bee impossible to ignore. Bright greens, reds, and oranges were especially popular.

Super Bee

The first sporty Coronet model, called the Super Bee, appeared in the late 1960s. People remember best, however, the 1970 version. The Coronet Super Bee had a huge 440-cubic-inch (7,210-cc) V-8 engine. Dodge made

UNDER THE SKIN

The Coronet's V-8 engine was known as "the Wedge" because of the way it is angled inside the car.

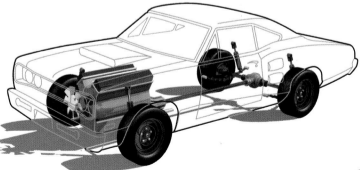

15

Ford Mustang Mach 1

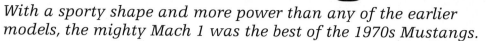

With a sporty shape and more power than any of the earlier models, the mighty Mach 1 was the best of the 1970s Mustangs.

The Mustang Mach 1 coupe was known as a "Sportsroof." Its roofline ran right into the back of the car.

In the 1970s, cars had big front bumpers for crash protection. Ford hid them well by painting them the same color as the body of the car.

The hood had two small scoops to feed extra cooling air to the engine.

The Mach 1 had a sports-style suspension to handle driving at great speeds.

Light-colored Mach 1s had black side stripes, while dark ones had white stripes.

Owners often added chrome alloy wheels and thick tires to the Mustang.

1969

The "Sportsroof" Mustangs make their first appearance.

1971

With its new body style, the Mustang Mach 1 is bigger, wider, and more powerful looking than earlier Mustangs.

F ord's Mustang had always sold well. For some people, however, Ford did not have a fast enough model among its cars, so they turned to **tuners** to improve performance. To compete with other fast cars of the time, Ford launched its own performance Mustang, the Mach 1.

among collectors today because of its size and great speed. The following year, fuel shortages led Ford to make a smaller, less powerful model.

Fast Performer

The Mach 1 remained at the top of the Mustang model line until 1974, when the company launched the Mustang Mk 2. The 1973 Mach 1 is the favorite Mustang

UNDER THE SKIN

The Mach 1 had a 302-cubic-inch (4,949-cc) V-8 engine that produced 136 horsepower.

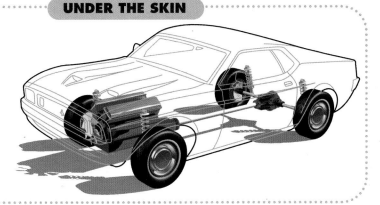

Ford Torino

The Torino coupe was longer, lower, wider, and more powerful than a Ford Mustang.

The black slats over the rear window prevented the sun from glaring at the driver following behind.

The Torino's big hood scoop was not just for show. The engine needed it for cooling at high speed.

Under the hood, the Torino had a 429-cubic-inch (7,030-cc) V-8 that produced 370 horsepower.

In the 1970s, Ford made this type of chrome hubcap standard on all of its models.

This Torino is a coupe. The Torino was also made as a four-door sedan and as a **station wagon.**

For drivers who found the Ford Mustang too small, the answer was the Ford Torino. Based on a similar design to the Mustang, the Torino was bigger all around, could carry up to five passengers in comfort, and also had a huge trunk.

Special Transmission

The model shown here is the Cobra, which was one of the most expensive and fastest Torinos. It was able to **accelerate** from 0 to 60 miles (96 kilometers) per hour in 5.9 seconds. It had a four-speed, stick-shift **transmission.** Its stick-shift transmission was unusual because most of its rivals had automatic transmissions.

A later type of Torino was the car used in the TV series and movie *Starsky and Hutch.*

1970
Ford releases its Torino for the 1970s. It is one of the biggest and widest cars on the road.

1974
The fuel crisis makes big V-8-powered coupes such as the Torino unpopular.

UNDER THE SKIN

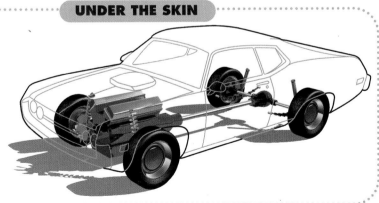

The track is the width of space between a car's wheels. The Torino's track was very wide, helping the car grip the road well at high speeds.

Mercury Capri 5.0L

Mercury's 1979 Capri model replaced the original Capri, which was built in 1969. It was based on the Ford Mustang.

The Capri's big trunk gave it plenty of luggage space.

The four-headlight front end had a plainer grille than the Mustang.

The Capri was only ever built as a hatchback. Ford did not want it to compete with its own soft-top Mustangs.

The Capri 5.0L had twin exhaust pipes for its V-8 engine.

From this angle, it is hard to tell the Capri apart from a 5.0-liter (305-cubic-inch) Ford Mustang. Only the headlights are different.

MILESTONES

1979

Mercury launches its new Capri. For the first time, a Capri has a hatchback.

1986

Following slow sales, Mercury withdraws the Capri from the market.

For most of the 1970s, Mercury, which is owned by Ford, made its Capri to compete with the Ford Mustang. Built in Germany, the car was popular in Europe. Versions of the Capri sold in the United States had 5.0-liter (305 cubic inch/4,999 cc) V-8 engines — larger than those sold in Europe.

New Model

In 1979, Mercury copied the Mustang to make its new Capri. Mercury kept the 5.0-liter V-8 engine — which gave the car the 5.0L name — but built the new Capri with a hatchback.

The Capri's styling was plain, but the car was also cheap. It appealed to buyers who wanted great performance without spending too much money.

UNDER THE SKIN

With its super-powerful V-8 engine, the Capri could accelerate from 0 to 60 miles (96 km) per hour in 6.5 seconds.

Oldsmobile Vista Cruiser

With a powerful engine and a big body, the Vista Cruiser was half muscle car, half station wagon.

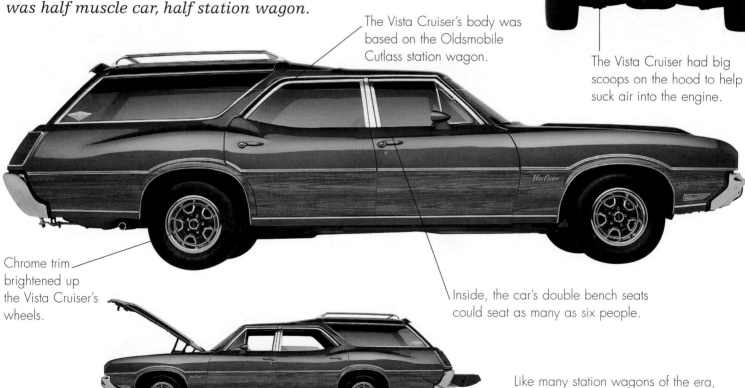

The Vista Cruiser's body was based on the Oldsmobile Cutlass station wagon.

The Vista Cruiser had big scoops on the hood to help suck air into the engine.

Chrome trim brightened up the Vista Cruiser's wheels.

Inside, the car's double bench seats could seat as many as six people.

Like many station wagons of the era, the bottom of the Vista Cruiser's body was covered with fake wood.

22

The Vista Cruiser could accelerate from 0 to 60 miles (96 km) per hour in less than six seconds.

1968

General Motors introduces the Oldsmobile Cutlass (pictured below). The Vista Cruiser is based on the Cutlass body frame and suspension.

1972

The Vista Cruiser is first built. It uses parts from the Cutlass and the Oldsmobile 4-4-2.

The Oldsmobile Vista Cruiser was based on two other Oldsmobile models. It had the best features of both of them. The body of the car came from an Oldsmobile Cutlass station wagon, right down to the fake wood panels along each side.

Powerful Station Wagon

Under the hood, however, the car had a huge 455-cubic-inch (7,456-cc) V-8 engine, which gave out a huge 300 horsepower. The engine and hood scoops were the same as those used on the Oldsmobile 4-4-2 muscle car.

UNDER THE SKIN

Despite the Vista Cruiser's big size, it had barely enough room under its hood for its massive V-8 engine.

Pontiac Firebird

The Pontiac Firebird was very popular.
It stayed in production for eleven years.

The twin hood scoops mark this Firebird out as a special edition "Formula" version.

The Firebird had steel "rally" wheels.

The Firebird's body was similar to the Chevrolet Camaro.

Firebirds had air conditioning, which made them popular in the hot Southern states.

To get around new rules about front fenders having to absorb the impact from a crash, the Firebird's nose was made out of collapsible plastic.

Extra body sections could be added to the Firebird to give it a wider, more muscular look.

1967
The first-generation Firebird (pictured below) makes its debut in February.

1979
The Firebird has its most successful year ever, with sales of more than 211,000.

In the 1970s, Pontiac made its sports cars smaller because of government rules. The Firebird was the most popular of its coupes. It stayed in production for eleven years with few changes. During that time, Pontiac sold more than two million Firebirds.

Endura Nose
The Firebird had a special front end called the Endura Nose. The Endura Nose was made out of plastic and could return to its original shape after low-speed crashes. Firebirds were well equipped for the time. Starting in the mid 1970s, buyers could order air-conditioning and a cassette player. The Firebird was always a good value for the money. It was also cheaper than the Chevrolet Camaro, which was a similar type of car.

UNDER THE SKIN

The Firebird's **axles** and engine were bolted onto the body of the car.

25

Pontiac Trans Am SD455

With 310 horsepower, the Trans Am SD455 was the most powerful Pontiac of the mid 1970s.

The SD455 had a big air scoop on the hood.

The trunk spoiler gave the car a cool, sporty look. It was attached to the trunk lid and lifted with it.

The steel wheels had chrome hubcaps that looked like alloy wheels.

For 1975, the Trans Am's rear-end styling was changed to include larger taillights.

The Firebird's cabin seat and door coverings were made of black plastic.

The special hood graphic on the Trans Am SD455 was called the "Screaming Eagle."

130 miles (209 km) per hour. The SD455 was sold in very small numbers and is a favorite among collectors today.

1969

Pontiac launches its first Trans Am.

1975

The Trans Am is redesigned with a new body style and a bigger engine.

Because of rising fuel prices and a shortage of oil, most people stopped wanting high-powered cars in the mid 1970s. Most of the major car makers scrapped the high-performance models from their lines.

But there were still some buyers who wanted a car that had the power to match the old muscle cars. So Pontiac made the Trans Am SD455. It had a huge 455-cubic-inch (7,456-cc) version of General Motors' famous V-8 engine, which helped it to go faster than

UNDER THE SKIN

The SD455 had a special suspension to help it deal with rough roads at high speeds.

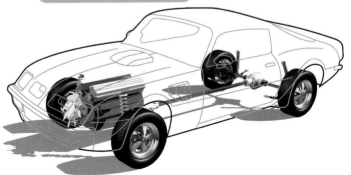

Pontiac Trans Am
10th Anniversary

To celebrate ten years of Trans Ams, Pontiac made this special edition model in silver.

The Trans Am shown here is a T-top. It had a bar down the middle of the roof between the two glass panels that made it look like there was a letter *T* on the car's roof. The panels could be removed on sunny days.

The front end of the Pontiac Trans Am 10th Anniversary was different from those seen on earlier Trans Ams. It had four square headlights and no grille.

The Trans Am had **disc brakes** on all four wheels. It could stop well at high speeds.

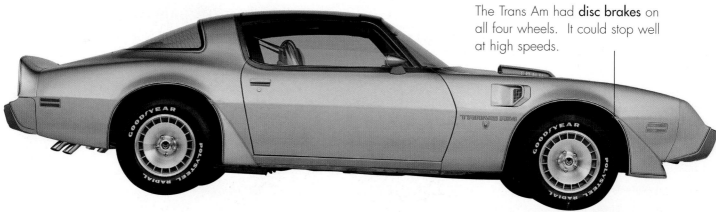

The 10th Anniversary Trans Am had silver paint and alloy wheels.

The Trans Am was always the top model in Pontiac's line of cars. To celebrate the car's success after ten years in production, Pontiac built a special silver edition. With its smooth, curvy lines, the anniversary model is now one of the most collectible cars of the late 1970s.

Special Edition
The 10th Anniversary Trans Am was special. As well as its silver paint job and big hood graphic, it had a silver leather interior and a dashboard with chrome details. It was also fitted with one-of-kind 15-inch (38-centimeter) **alloy** wheels and a wide body to make it stand out from the ordinary Trans Am models.

UNDER THE SKIN

The SD455 could accelerate from 0 to 60 miles (96 km) per hour in just 5.2 seconds.

Glossary

accelerate to increase speed

aerodynamic having smooth, sleek surfaces around which air easily flows

alloy two or more metals mixed together

axle shafts on which a wheel, or pair of wheels, revolves

chassis the part of a car body to which the engine, transmission, and suspension are attached

classic something with lasting appeal

convertible a car with a roof that can be lowered

coupe a two-door car, usually seating only two people

cylinder a chamber inside the engine where a piston is forced up and down by burning gas to create power

disc brakes brakes that work by pressing a metal plate against rubber pads to slow the car down

drag racers people who take part in drag races, a competition to see which car accelerates the fastest

exhaust pipes metal tubes that take the gasses resulting from burned fuel away from an engine and make it quieter

fiberglass a lightweight material made from glass strands and plastic

Formula One having to do with Formula One races; Formula One races take place over an entire weekend, with practice sessions on Friday, two practice sessions and a qualifying session on Saturday, and the race itself on Sunday

fuel injection a system used in most modern engines that sprays the fuel directly into the engine, improving power

grille a guard at the front end of the car that lets in air to cool the engine

hatchback a car with a door on the rear that opens into a storage area

horsepower a unit of measure of the power of an engine

muscle car an American-made, two-door sports car with a powerful engine for high-performance driving

NASCAR National Association for Stock Car Racing

sedan a closed automobile having two or four doors and front and rear seats

shock absorbers devices fitted to a car that make it a smoother ride on bumpy surfaces

station wagon a long car with extra storage space and windows at the rear in place of a trunk

suspension a system of springs at the base of a car's body that keeps the car even on bumpy surfaces

transmission a system in a vehicle that controls its gears, sending power from the engine to the wheels to make them move

trim decorative parts of a car, such as moldings, fenders, and hub caps

tuners people who improve car engines to make them perform better and drive faster

V-8 describes engines that have eight cylinders placed opposite each other in a V-shape

vents slits or openings that take in or let out air or fumes

For More Information

Books

American Muscle Cars, 1960–1975. Cars & Trucks (series). Bruce LaFontaine (Dover Publications)

Big Book of Cars. (DK Publishing)

Car. DK Eyewitness (series). Richard Sutton and Elizabeth Baquedano (DK Children)

Cars. All About (series). Peter Harrison (Southwater)

Muscle Cars. Automania! (series). Katherine Bailey (Crabtree Publishing Company)

Street Power. Hot Wheels (series). Bill Coulter (Motorbooks International)

The Story of the Ford Mustang. Classic Cars (series). Jim Mezzanotte (Gareth Stevens Publishing)

Web Sites

All Muscle Cars
www.allmusclecars.com

Dearborn Classics
www.dearbornclassics.com/torino.html

Museum of Automobile History
www.themuseumofautomobilehistory.com

StarskyTorino.com
www.starskytorino.com

Publishers note to educators and parents:
Our editors have carefully reviewed these Web sites to ensure that they are suitable for children. Many Web sites change frequently, however, and we cannot guarantee that a site's future contents will continue to meet our high standards of quality and educational value. Be advised that children should be closely supervised whenever they access the Internet.

Index